Under the Act:
Protected

Under the Act:
Protected

Willie Thaiday

Damien Writer, Delphine Geia, Lillian Geia & Cathy Dyball

Indigenous Publishing
2017

First Printing: 1981

ISBN: 978-0-6481006-1-4

Indigenous Publishing
PO Box 7173
Garbutt, QLD
4814

www.indigenouspublishing.com

Dedication

DEDICATED TO THE PEOPLE OF PALM ISLAND, TO THOSE THAT WERE THROWN OFF AND TO THOSE STILL THERE.

Thaiday Family, Townsville, 1964

Back Row (Left to Right): David, Theresa, Willie, Dulcie (Sister Loyola Mary), Madge, Bill, and Telly. Front Row (Left to Right): Joshua, Selina, Aloysius, Patrick (grandson), and Michael. Absent: Nina

Electra Head

Hayman Rock

South East Cape

Paluma Rock

White Rock o
S.I. 1.3994
O. 2. 0
Owl.1.417

Chilcott Rocks •

NORTH EAST
(DTHOORAKOOL)
BAY

BARBER I
(BOODTHEAN)

1498

G.G. 1873 .1 .1834
Owl. 1166

Reserve for The Benefit of the Aboriginal Inhabitants of the State

Fawn Hd

Elk Cliff

BULLIMBOOROO
BAY

GREAT PALM
ISLAND

R.216 (pt)
Res. 925

MT. BENTLEY
1816

974

The Casements

1283

Sibauia Pt.

NUMBUILABUDGEE
BAY

Wallaby Pt
(Guaree)

BUTLER BAY
(BURRUMBROO)

Miranda Pt

COOLGAREE BAY

•Part of R.216
Lazaret for the reception
and medical treatment
of lepers
G.G. 1887 .1 .1490

Calliope Channel
(Bulgoonia)
Wallaby Pt
(Bulgoonia)

CURACOA I
(NOOGOO)

R.216(pt)
(NOOGOO)

971

P   A   L   M

COOLGOOD BAY
SEE
INSET

(GOWYAROWA)
CHALLENGER
BAY

REGINA BAY

CASEMENT BAY

FANTOME
(EUMILLI)
ISLAND

PENCIL BAY

Steamer
Passage

R.216 (pt)
ECLIPSE I
(GAROGUBBEE)
206

R.216 (pt)
BRISK I
(CULGAROOL)
229

for the reception
and medical
treatment of
lepers

Health Purps R.
890. 0. 0
G.G. 1941.2. 1076

JUNO
BAY

R.436
7117

8
R.436

R.436
7118

724

680

Health Purps Res.
1080. 0. 0
G.G. 1941.2. 1076

G.G. 1960
1.1166

5360
(In Res.
In Por.19)
808

R.216 (pt)
FALCON I
(GABOORO)
104

R.216 (pt)
ESK I
166
(BOOPUND)

Dido
Rock

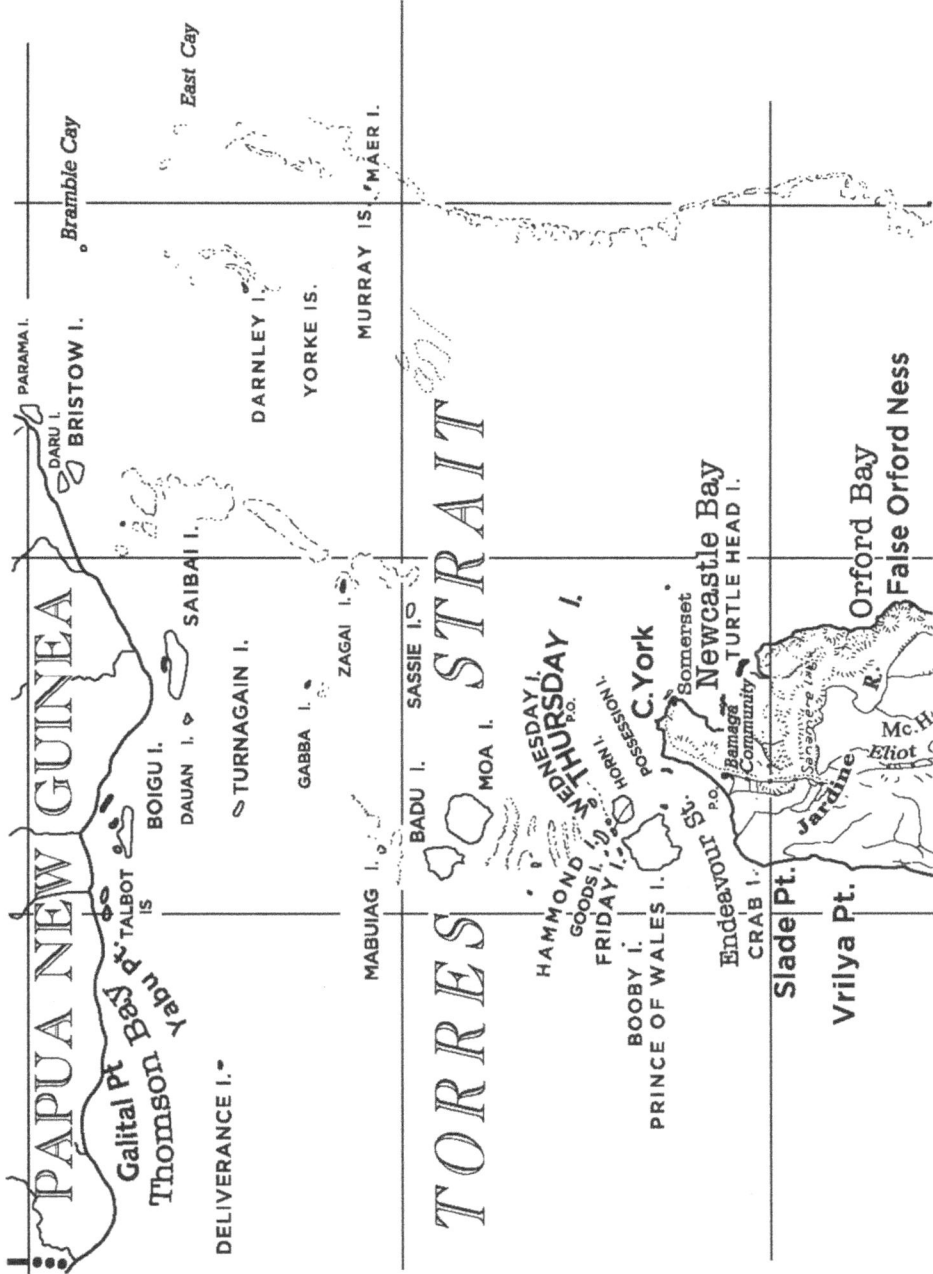

PAPUA NEW GUINEA

Galital Pt
Thomson Bay
Yaru Pt
TALBOT
IS

PARAMA I.
DARU I.
BRISTOW I.

East Cay

Bramble Cay

DELIVERANCE I.

BOIGU I.
DAUAN I.
SAIBAI I.
TURNAGAIN I.
GABBA I.
ZAGAI I.

MÄER I.
MURRAY IS.
YORKE IS.
DARNLEY I.

MABUIAG I.
BADU I.
SASSIE I.
MOA I.

TORRES STRAIT

HAMMOND I.
GOODS I.
FRIDAY I.
BOOBY I.
PRINCE OF WALES I.

WEDNESDAY I.
THURSDAY I.
P.O.
HORN I.
POSSESSION I.
Endeavour St.
CRAB I.

C. York
Somerset
Newcastle Bay
TURTLE HEAD I.

Bamaga
Community
P.O.
Jardine
R.
Eliot
Mc.H

Slade Pt.
Vrilya Pt.

Orford Bay
False Orford Ness

CONTENTS

Foreword

As Strike '57 marks its 60th anniversary it is important this story is retold so that people appreciate the significance of young Palm Islanders stand against the oppressive Queensland Government of that time.

The Palm Island strike in 1957 was one of the early defining events in the struggle for recognition of Aboriginal rights in Australia. The leadership of these Palm Islanders inspired a generation to demand justice and to work for reform of draconian laws.

I myself was privileged to meet and talk with a number of these young men in the 1960s and their words impressed on me the need to document the history of **Aboriginal** conflict.

The determination of Albert Geia and his co-workers continues to remind Indigenous Australians that it is still necessary that any type of discrimination be challenged.

"Under the Act " must be widely read so that we all recognise and pay tribute to those Palm Islanders who not only challenged the laws of the 1950s but set a foundation standard of equality for future generations.

Henry Reynolds

INTRODUCTION

Legislation specifically for Aborigines and Islanders in Queensland dates back to the Native Labourer's Protection Act of 1884. Its purpose was to protect natives against "black birding" for use as slave labor on ships, especially in the pearl-shell and beche der mer fishing industries.

In 1897 the Aboriginals Protection and Restriction of the Sale of Opium Act was proclaimed and this remained in force with successive amendments until 1939. It provided further protection for Aborigines against exploitation as slave labour, especially in the fishing industry but also later on in the pastoral industry. The restriction of the sale of opium was included because it fitted a context where the supply of liquor and opium to Aboriginals was prohibited. At the same time there was the attempt to restrict the opium trade generally.

Protectors, usually local police officers, were appointed for each district where there were Aboriginals. The Protector's permission was required for an aboriginal to be employed. Such permission could be revoked at any time. Aboriginals in employment were under the supervision of the Protector. The Protector could remove aboriginals to reserves. Without the Protector's permission aboriginals could not be removed from one district to another. The Protector's permission was required for a female aboriginal to marry anyone other than an aboriginal. The protector could remove aboriginal camps from towns to whatever distance he liked. The Protector could order aboriginal medical examinations. Every aboriginal who left his native place to work on a ship had to be medically examined for contagious disease when he returned. An aboriginal will was invalid unless approved and witnessed by the Protector.

It was an offence for aboriginals to possess liquor or opium. An aboriginal could be sent to an institution if in the Minister's opinion he was uncontrollable. The Protector "shall undertake the general care, protection and management of the property of all aboriginals in the district assigned to him."

Where people became exempt from the Act that person's money and property could remain in the control of the Protector. Wages of aboriginals were paid to the Protector, who could also impose summary punishment of up to fourteen days imprisonment for various offences.

All articles (blankets, clothing etc.) distributed to aboriginals remain the property of the Crown. All letters written by aboriginals on reserves or in institutions must go to the superintendent or officer in charge who could withhold them from transmission and return them to the writers.

Aboriginal reserves, created under the Land Act as land reserved from sale or lease for the use and enjoyment by aboriginals, were under the control of the protector and settlements on reserves under the control of Superintendants Inmates (sic) were required to obey all intructions, to work without pay for at least 24 hours per week. They could be summarily punished with 14 days imprisonment for any crime, serious misconduct, neglect of duty, gross insubordination or breach of rules and corporal punishment could be inflicted on those under sixteen for similar offences.

In 1939 the legislation was overhauled and the Aborigines Preservation and Protection Act, and the Torres Strait Islanders Acts, together with their regulations, replaced the old Act. The Chief Protector became the Director of Native Affairs but the system of protectors in each district and superintendents on reserves remained the same. The Director could remove Aboriginals to reserves, release them from reserves and remove them from one reserve to another. While retaining the old provisions designed to protect aboriginals against exploitation in employment the new Act spelt out in great detail provisions for running reserves. The regulations under the Act ran to eleven pages of the Queensland Government Gazette of April 23rd 1945. Regulations dealing specifically with reserves ran to three and a half pages. Some of them went as follows:

R 22:   A protector or superintendent shall have power to prohibit in writing, the playing of any game, whether played with cards or otherwise however (hereinafter called a prohibited game) on a reserve, settlement or mission reserve under his supervision; any person found guilty of playing any such game shall be guilty of an offence.

R 18:   Every aboriginal on a reserve, settlement or mission reserve shall obey all lawful orders of the protector or superintendent and other officers of such reserve, settlement or mission reserve.

R 24(1): The protector of a reserve, settlement or mission reserve may direct an aboriginal to deliver to him anything which is in the possession or at the disposal of the said aboriginal and which in the opinion of the protector or superintendent is likely to be the subject or cause of a disturbance of the harmony good order or discipline of the reserve, settlement or mission reserve.

R 28 (1): Every aboriginal shall, when required by the protector or superintendant, perform, according to his ability, any work necessary for the development and maintenance of the reserve, settlement or mission reserve as directed by the protector or superintendent; provided that an aboriginal shall not be called upon to work in excess of thirty-two hours in any one week without remuneration.

19.   S22,   1939

R 28 (2) Every aboriginal who, without reasonable excuse, proof of which shall lie upon him, refuses to work when required to do so by the protector or superintendent or any officer under his direction, or found to be evading such work, shall be guilty of an offence.

4

Form No. 6
  "The Aboriginals Preservation and Protection Act of 1939"
  Scale of Rations for Settlement Inmates.

Item		Men	Women	Children under 5 years including all Dorm Inmates.
		Oz.	Oz.	Oz.
Beef – non-working or part time working inmates.	daily	4 4/7	4 4/7	2 2/7
Full time working inmates		16	12	
Flour (wholemeal)	daily	16	16	8
Oatmeal (or 1st break wheat)	daily	1	1	1
Rice	weekly	4	4	4
Sago	weekly	2	2	2
Sugar	daily	2	2	2
Syrup	weekly	8	8	8
Green Peas	weekly	4	4	4
Split Peas	weekly	2	2	1
Tea	daily	¼	¼	¼
Cream of Tartar				2lb per 150lb of flour
Soda				1lb per 150lb of flour
Barley	weekly	1	1	1
Fine Salt				As required
Washing Soda				As required
Tobacco (working inmates)	weekly	2	1 1/2	
Bars of soap	weekly	1/8 bar	1/8 bar	1/8 bar
Dripping	weekly	2	2	2
Milk (Fresh)*			½ Pint	1 Pint

*When fresh milk is not available it is to be replaced by full cream powdered milk to normal strength of fresh milk.

Form No. 4
"The Aboriginal Preservation and Protection Act of 1939"

Permit for the celebration of the Marriage of an Aboriginal with a Person other than an Aboriginal

Permission by Director,

I, ... Director of Native Affairs in the State of Queensland, hereby give permission, by virtue of section 19 of the said Act, for the celebration of the marriage of ...., a female/male person who is an aboriginal within the meaning of the said Act to

, a female/male person who is not an Aboriginal within the meaning of the said Act.

Dated this   day of   , 19   .

Director of Native Affairs.

Permission by authorized protector.

I,   , being a protector of aboriginals for the district of

in the State of Queensland, being especially authorized herein by the marriage of an aboriginal with a person other than an aboriginal, hereby give permission for the celebration of the marriage of   , a female/male person who is not an aboriginal within the meaning of the said Act, to   a female/male person who is not an aboriginal within the meaning of the said Act.

Dated this   day of   , 19   .

Protector of Aboriginals.

The special authority referred to above is to be attached to this document.

Form No. 4A.

"The Aboriginals Preservation and Protection Act of 1939"
Permit for the Celebration of Marriage between Aboriginals.
I,   Director of Native Affairs/Protector
of Aboriginals for the district of   (or
*superintendent)
of the settlement or reserve   ),
hereby give permission
by virtue of section of the abovementioned Act, for the
celebration of the marriage of the male   , to
the female
(who resides in the said district * settlement or mission
reserve), the said persons being aboriginals within the meaning of
the said Act.

Dated this   day of   , in the year

.

*Strike out what is not applicable.
Protector of Aboriginals
Superintendent of a Settlement
or Mission Reserve

The Torres Strait Islanders Act of 1939 was more concerned to provide for local government of the island reserves by the island councils themselves, always subject to the Director of Native Affairs and the Protector.

These Acts remained in force until 1965 when the Aborigines and Torres Strait Islands Affairs Act was passed. Under this Act the Protectorate was abolished and nearly all the provisions relating to people living off reserves repealed. In 1971 the Acts were divided again between aboriginals and islanders and now apply almost entirely to the administration and local government of reserves. The Director, now the director of Aboriginal and Islander Advancement, still retains control of the reserves and exercises this control through the system of managers and officers of his department which run the reserves. The reserve councils have gradually been given more authority in the running of the reserves but they have neither the personnel nor the resources to fulfil their purpose as local governing bodies.

What began as an attempt to protect aboriginals against exploitation in employment gradually changed to total control of every facet of their lives on and off reserves; what began as strict provisions for wages and conditions finished under the 1939 Act with a situation where aboriginals could be forced to work for thirty-two hours a week without pay; what began as an attempt to enable aboriginals to participate with equality in the economic life of the nation finished with regulations fitting for prisons.

This then is the background to Willie's story which was told to me during conversations in June 1979. When I first heard I thought that here was a classic case of a life lived under the Aborigines Act of Queensland. The story therefore had obvious political import and for that reason should be made more widely available so that non Aborigines would understand what life under the Act was like and so that later generations of Aborigines and Islanders, who hopefully live in happier circumstances, would have a written record of the lives of their forefathers.

I also thought that the story would need considerable editing and adaptation before it could be published.

However, as the story unfolded, it became clear that the political import of the story, although considerable, was none the

less secondary. For what we have here is the record of the life of a priceless human spirit which flourished in the midst of the most outrageous humiliation and assault on human dignity which this country could perpetrate. The story is that of a man who was exiled three times in his life but whose spirit was never broken and whose interest in and grip on life is still as strong as it was the day he dived from the military patrol boat during the second world war because he was refused enlistment into the army for being an Aboriginal from Palm Island.

I also found that the story could be told best in Willie's own words and I fear that the slight changes I made in the way of removing repetitious pieces and endeavoring to order the material somewhat may already have detracted from the impact of Willie's account.

This is a tale of human struggle against oppression with all the ambiguities which attend those concepts and although it is an interesting enough exercise to try to analyze those concepts we should not allow that preoccupation to blind us to the personality and the inherent greatness of the person whose story this is.

Patrick Mullins   S.J.
Townsville
November, 1979

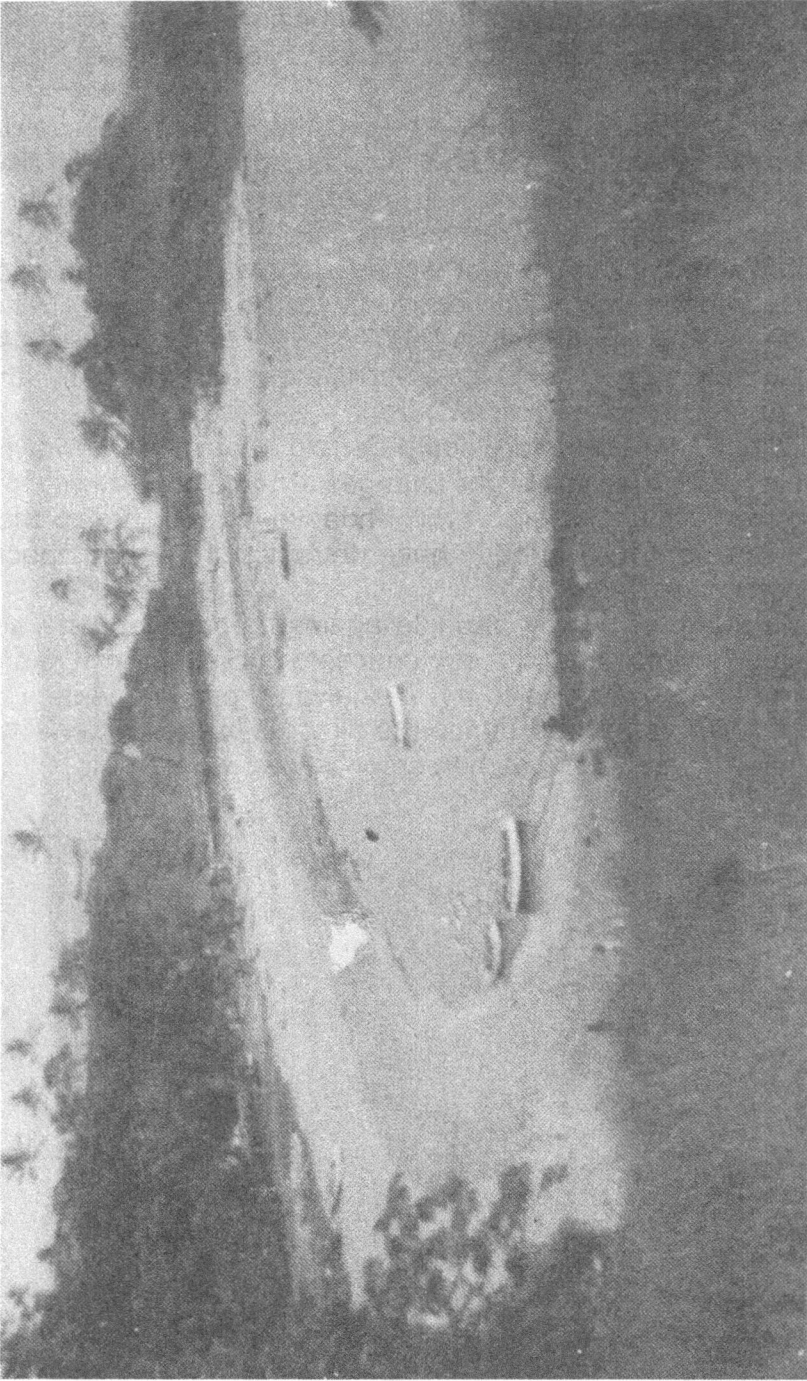

Darnley Island (Late 1940's)

Medigee Village, Darnley Island

CHAPTER ONE:

DARNLEY ISLAND TO PALM ISLAND

My name is Willie Thaiday: Island name is Willie Sinaiya.
I was born Darnley Island 1913, 18th December. Educated at school on Darnley up to the fourth grade. That is all they allow me.

In 1925 or 26 we have teacher from Scotland. His name is Mr. McIntosh Murray. One day he ask all the boys if we can start a scout movement.

We say: "What is scout movement? We never seen one."
At last he show me photo of white scout in England. When he show me photo we agree because they got good uniform, them young boys. He is in photograph himself, standing with young boys. Anyway we agree and we all join in to make Scout movement on Darnley.

To get our own uniform we got to produce our own money so we go out to work for fellows who invite us in the village. There are twelve of us. When we work for a day they give us a pound. Another fellow come and we go and make a pig sty for him. We do all them things – dig wells, carry sand and stones, do anything for anybody in the village when they ask us. We also go out and dive for Trochus Shells: we scrape and dry coconuts or beat them and spread them out to sea along the reef. When grease go all around we see the Trochus Shells laying down we dive to them. When we pick them up we fill one or two bags and Mr. Murray take them to Thursday Island to sell them for us. In no time we make enough money for uniforms and then Mr. Murray ask if we like to be sea scouts.

We say: "Yes, that would do us nice, we Islanders.

We join the sea scouts and all go out in a boat in our spare time. We borrow the lugger and go out; we use the sailing boat; getting very good now. Then I left school that year, about 1928, and we stop.

I work on a boat for one year on the island; 1929 I work in the island and in 1930 I came down south on a boat, far as Cairns.

After Christmas back home we recruit again for another boat called Erub. That is native for Darnley name; the boat belong to Darnley. Skipper is Douglas Pitt, a very good skipper too. I go back home after twelve months on the boat to have another Christmas at home. After Christmas trouble crop up on the island.

During the night when there was a big native island dance for Christmas one boy make trouble and we all fall in. Trouble is with a young girl from a different island and three of us seem to be responsible. I am so young that I can't speak English and the Protector is a very rough man. He believe what the council tell him.

The council never stick up for any young fellow – they always like to shove them in gaol.

All right, the three of us go to gaol and the next morning they pull us out and put us in court. Mr. Green say: "You boys got to go to Palm Island."

We didn't know what to say. No matter if you plead not guilty you are still guilty with him. A lugger was there, Adelia, belong to Mr. Morey from Thursday Island.

He say: "Now you boys go in the boat and stay there. We can't hold you in gaol here. Go in the boat until three week's time: Then I will send you to Thursday Island. You are not allowed to come ashore, not allowed to see your mother, father or family."

We stay in the boat. My sister got engaged one day but I am not allowed to go for the feast.

After three weeks they send us to Thursday Island. When we come to Thursday Island we think we will get sent direct to Palm Island but Mr. Green say: "I will send you to Palm Island now. Go on the steamer, the Wandana, and; you can sign on any lugger for down south. When you get to Townsville or Palm Island they can discharge you there after twelve months." We say: "All right."

I go and sign on with Mr. Hocking, a big business man on Thursday Island and I go on a boat called Eron with a Japanese skipper called Kajishi. We leave Thursday Island in February and sail down south to start work.

We start out in northerly direction outside Cooktown and work for twelve months. The skipper like me very much so he don't leave me on Palm Island but while we are on Eron we call there twice and when I see it I say: "That's the place we gonna come to." But instead at Christmas time Kajishi take me right back to Thursday Island. The other two boys were on different boat but they come back to Thursday Island too. We meet there, get discharge about Christmas time and go home for Christmas.

The skipper tell me: "Well, Willie, by the time we get to Thursday Island I think all the trouble will be over. They will send you home instead of Palm Island."

I say: "They might too."

When we go to Thursday Island we are happy to be home, happy to see Darnley again but Mr. Hocking ring the courthouse. He say: "What do I have to do?"

Send the boys back to Darnley or what." They say: "Which boys?"

He call our names. "Oh no, they should be sent to Palm Island. Anyway I will send a policeman there to pick them up."

That's too bad. After twelve months away I have to go to gaol and then come back to Palm Island. We never go to Darnley again, never see our mother again.

That evening the policemen come, Mr. Toad and Mr. Grunt. Mr. Toad is a very rough man at Thursday Island. We see the

police truck pull up and Mr. Grunt and Mr. Toad come out. "Them three boys from Eron here?" they say

"All right, come on, get your ports." We take our ports. They gonna put us in goal and send us to Palm Island. Ah gee, bad luck.

Anyway we get in the truck and they take us and lock us up. We stay in number nine room, way inside, very dark. Anyone would think we are murderers. I never forget it.

We stay three nights while the Wandana go to Burketown. Next morning we get up at about eight o'clock. I can hear the steamer whistle at Doctor Point – The Wandana. I say: "By gee, thank God we are gonna get out from this gaol anyway, No matter where we go. We can go back to Palm Island so long as we get out from this number nine room, this cell."

That evening Mr. Toad come round: "right ho, you boys, get your ports ready. You gonna go on Wandana now. I send you to Palm Island." He thought we were worrying but I was feeling glad all the time.

When the truck come we get our ports and go down to the jetty. At the jetty I see a big crowd of people. They always come down to the jetty to see the steamer. So we come, get off there, walk along the jetty and get on steamer. When we get on the boat I was very pleased to get away from that place. We stand on the deck. Next minute the skipper blow the whistle, the Wandana move and we set off for Cairns.

We sail all that night and the next day. Nobody escort us on the Wandana. If we like to escape, run away on a boat we can because there are lot of boats, fishing boats from the other islands stationed out there. They get their stuff from the steamer. But we don't bother to run away.

We come to Coen. There we pick up one policeman but he say nothing. I tell my mates: "I think that is a young policeman. I know from the way he look." Anyway we come all the way free to Cairns.

The sergeant of police meet us there but he don't talk to us – he talk to the other policeman. He give him something, a letter. Then we are ready to go, the policeman come around and say, "You boys going to Palm Island?' We say: "Yes" He say: "Well, I am escorting you now. You will be alright; don't worry." "Have you been to Palm Island before?" I say: "Yes" He is a very nice policeman; young fellow too; him and his wife.

We came to Cairns and we see police cars, two or three of them, all full of policemen. When we get to the wharf we get off right into police hands. The young policeman let us off there and another policeman is in control of us. We drive around to the police station to get locked up. At supper time he let us out but at night time he put us back in again. That was Christmas Eve. After supper we listen to all the Christmas carols. By gee, it break our hearts.

Anyway we sleep and next morning a policeman knock on the door: "Come on you boys, you got to get train for Townsville today."

The same young policeman come along. He got to go to Brisbane for his holidays. He come and say: "All you boys ready?" We jump in and catch the train from Cairns. He tell us: "No need to be frightened. I been away for four years, never had a Christmas at home." He take us to Townsville.

When we come to Townsville the police are there again. By gee, we are in police hands all the way. They take us to the watch house but when they take us there I see some Palm Island people and I know them. We all know them and that make our hearts glad. There are some young girls there too and that take our minds off all our sorrows about Palm Island so we forget. I know one girl who got married to Kitchener Bligh – her name is Mable Ahkee.

We sleep there and next day he take us to the boat, the cargo boat, which run back and forward from Palm Island to Townsville, Townsville to Palm Island, twice a week. We get on that boat and leave for Palm Island. It is nine o'clock in the morning. When we come out we pull up the sail. The skipper is Mr. Hamilton.

We expect nothing at Palm Island no people there to see us. The first time we come as free people working on a boat but this time we come as prisoners. When we get there it is 4 o'clock in the afternoon and there is a big king tide.

Mr. Hamilton take the boat right up to the shore. I listen and hear a little boy call out my name – Monty Pryor – he was 10 years old then. Wilfred Obah and some other little boys are there too.

When we jump off, we jump right into police hands again, native police this time. Tommy King, sergeant, is from Bowen; Arthur Gall, a rough man, from Coen; and Mick O'Brien, another tough old guy, from out west, Biloela or somewhere.

Adult Spear Thrower from Mapoon
Child: Jack Ebagoola at Townsville Sports Reserve.
(late 1920's or early 1930's)

Mapoon Dancers, sent to Palm Island, performing at Townsville Sports Reserve.
(late 1920's or early 1930's)

CHAPTER TWO:

PALM ISLAND (part one)

We land at Palm Island close to New Year, December 27th, 1932.

We see many people there, about 1500, and 25 police are there ready to arrest us. The superintendent is Mr. Delaney and there is a rule there that you go to the office and open your port so they can find out what you got.

The policeman escort us to see Mr. Delaney. Mr. Delaney say: "You boys must come to office." So we go to office and he say: "Right ho boys, open your ports." We got to look what you got." My cousin, Lui George, and Lorbrey Sailor are there.

They find nothing in my port or Lorbrey's but in Lui's port they find girl medicine. They do not know what it is but there are many old people there who talk among themselves. They know what it is, they call it Mussin. Mr. Delaney call us over.

I say: "I got nothing." Lorbrey say he got nothing but Lui say: "That's mine." Mr. Delaney say: "What you want woman medicine for?" Lui say: "That not woman medicine. We use that to make our hair grow."

How he change his mind so quick, I don't know, but Mr. Delaney believe him straight away. He say: "Oh well, that is nothing." The policeman get very wild because they know it is girl medicine but Mr. Delaney say: "You can take it home." Then Mr. Delaney ask us: "You know anybody here?" We say that we know Mundy William, one of our countrymen, an old fellow. He say yes, he got plenty of room but he got no room at all. His house is very small. He only pleased to have his own countrymen there. Anyway we stop there through Christmas holidays.

When work start, Mr. Delaney say: "I want to see them three Island boys." Sergeant Tommy King bring us to the office and Mr. Delaney say: "I warn you now. While you are on this place you are not to muck around with married women; you are not to play around with single girls; you got to obey the rules and listen to what the sergeant here say." We say: "Yes, we understand."

He say: "Now I am going to put you on the gang belong to Jimmy Harvey." So we go on Jimmy Harvey's gang.

Palm Island was not much then – only half a dozen houses with iron on the tops, all the rest are grass houses. Jimmy Harvey got a big gang and we go out to pull the bladey grass for the houses. The old people build the houses and we get the grass for them.

One morning nearly a murder take place where we are pulling the bladey grass. A bloke called Paddy Leonard hit Nundi Bamboo with a tomahawk. They are two countrymen from Bloomfield River. They get a set on one another up there and couldn't settle it back home. Anyway Jimmy Harvey take us with him to court in Townsville and he speak for all the gang. We stay there about three or four weeks and one of our boys make trouble. "Right ho, you boys, you all got to go to the farm for three or four weeks." But we all not make trouble, only one of us, and I say that we are not going to take punishment like that.

When we go there are a lot of old people, Weipa people, all in a very old house and they say: "You can go in the house too." Them old people spit. A habit they have and sometimes they spit on you. We stop there for two weeks and start to grow ring worms all over the body. I think all the time: "We can only get free from here if a boat come, the lugger from Thursday Island." Only we are not allowed to go into the settlement.

We are working on the road to Doctor Point. There is a good road there now but before the war there was no road. You can't drive a dray there because the bullocks sway over the big rocks. We drill through the rocks, blow them with dynamite. We work like anything, we slave. A bloke called Vincent Blackman is the head ganger with Jack Davidson, both from Cherbourg settlement. They make us work.

No money - we only get tobacco, not allowed good tobacco –
Mareeba, Talisman or Waratah.

One evening we see a white sail between Phantom Island
and Curacoa. We were glad. The skipper is Kosaka – I work for
him before and he come to Palm Island to pick me up because
he know I stay there. I was very good boy for him.

He come and ask the super: "Can I have them Island boys
for my crew?" Super say: "No, you can't have them. They are on
punishment." If you want them you can have one or two; you
can't have them all."

So he say: "Can I have Willie and Emery Mooka?" Emery go
to Mr. Delaney and Mr. Delaney say: "Yes you can go." So we
sign on and leave on the Waikato.

We work very hard, go as far as Mackay, then up to Cairns,
then back at Christmas time to Palm Island. This time we got to
go over to Phantom, get examined, get blood test for Leprosy
and V.D. You got to stop there two or three weeks but while you
are there they don't just leave you there, you got to work. Uncle
Genemi Geia, Eva's[1] father-in-law say: "You stay with me." We
couldn't stay anywhere else because there are too many flies on
Phantom Island and you can't go anywhere on the island, only
round the front. Anyway a fellow called George Parker examine
us and say: "You are alright; you can go to Palm tomorrow."

Next day we leave that place and go to Palm Island. We
were happy to be there again.

We stay there for a while, working on a little cutter diving for
trochus shells round the island – Barber Bay, North East Bay,
Pencil Bay, Canon Bay, North Palm, Curacoa and Phantom. We
go every week and come in on the weekends.
We get no pay – only tucker and tobacco. We stay there up
to New Year 1934. Then another boat sail in.

This time it is a lugger called Waipa with a Japanese skipper called Maize. Some of the crew know me and they say to Maize: "you go ask Willie." So Maize go to office and say: "I want Willie." I feel glad again because I am going away. He sign me on and take me out again. We go the same way, on Swan reef, right out to the ocean and way down outside Green Island. We go in every three months, stop a fortnight, then out again for another three months.

Mr O'Leary[2] say we are free now, free to go home or stop there so when we get to Cairns them boys say; "Come on, we take you home to Darnley." They take my port and hide it from me but I want to go back to Palm Island. I didn't want to go to Darnley. That would be no use because they already sent me from there. Better I stop here.

Early in the morning, when I hear the Windlass I jump from the lugger, push off in the dinghy and go to the jetty. While I walk the jetty one of the boys come, take the dinghy back to the boat and they sail off across the harbour.

The day after Christmas I go to see the policeman. He say: "Where you from?" I say: "Palm Island". "But you're Island boy." I say: "I went there three years ago." "All right, we will send you to Palm Island by train. Get your port and go outside. You're free but tomorrow morning don't miss the train. It goes from Cairns at 8 o'clock." They let me sleep on the verandah of the gaol house; the policeman run me over in the morning; they got my ticket and I come to Townsville.

On the lugger we get ten shillings a week, two pounds a month and it was paid to the police. When we want the money we got to go and get it but they only allow you an advance, one pound at a time. We can't go by ourselves because by ourselves they won't believe us. We got to go with the skipper, our agent. Only one pound for three weeks in the harbour and you can't go back for another pound. When one pound is gone you don't get no more.

Our wages come up to three pounds a month so then we say: "Send the money to our mothers." Our mothers draw one pound at home while we have two pounds.

When I come back to Palm Island I say: "I been roaming around too much. I think I will settle down." Then I get married, March 14th 1936. My wife was only sixteen and I was twenty three. Me and Mick Miller got married the same day and we been very good friends ever since. Before we get married, when I am only engaged, I don't want to go out on dinghy and dive. We only work for nothing. We got to go round the island, pull the dinghy all the time. You pick up the shells all right but the government take them. We get nothing for it. We only get tobacco and we make damper and doboy (dumpling). That's all we eat so I refuse to go diving. A bloke called Mr Prior, temporary superintendant say: "You refuse to go round there to dive. Okay I send you to Mundy Bay, to George Watson's gang, cutting timber."

So I go around there cutting timber. We go to Barber Bay cutting pine trees. We cut a swag from there every Monday and every Monday we walk nine miles over them logs, right up to Barber Bay, where they call it Carpet Snake Creek. We camp there inside Barber Island and we cut big pines. We go on top and push all the big pine down about five, six or seven hundred yards we bark the pine so we can push them down. We cut the pine and shoot them down into the water, use them as floaters.

We bore holes, take them to Carpet Snake Creek, anchor them there while we wait for the launch to come on Friday morning to take the logs to the mill.

In them times it was really hard but you got to keep it up. Six or seven logs at a time; you got to shift them all the time because if you let them dry the rope break. We were like that for three or four months. Only get tobacco, flour and rice – no money.

28

We work at Barber Bay but I left the wife at Butler Bay. When three months is up we come back to Mundy Bay – team of bullocks work there. My father in law himself drive the bullocks. We come from Barber Bay doing all right too.

We used to load the wagons at Butler Bay with all the logs from up on the hill, Mundy Bay Hill. They call it Old Camp but we call it Mountain Home.

Timber used to come in Butler Bay and Barber Bay and we shoot them down a big shute there. They got to come through on a big long shute and some timber go round to Mundy Bay. The bullocks go round, pick them up and shoot them down again. The logs are big – take six teams, five teams or four teams. We drag them down to the Catholic Mission and dump the sinkers. The floaters have to lay out on beach before we take them round to the mill.

My father in law say: "I got to go for holidays. You like to take the gang?" I say: "Yes, I take the gang all right but I only been here two years. Lot of fellows understand timber more than I do." He say: "Doesn't matter, you can work there."

He take my wife and small kids to Millaa Millaa and I stay there looking after the gang, big gang. While working I get experience all the time. Wagons come from farm, load them up and dump them at Missionary Bay.

That's all the work on Palm Island. We only work for tobacco.

In 1936, just after I get married, they decide to elect a council, the first council on Palm Island. I was elected. There is me, Alby Kyle, Sid Cerico, Fred Braickenbridge and Percy Smallwood. George Ryan was our secretary. We get no wages for it. One day I tell the council: "I think good idea if we try to see the government, see if they can give us wages."

We work a long time just for tobacco, not good tobacco either. We say we will try to get some kind of wages, something for the work we done so go to Mr. Simple[3] about wages.

Mr. Simple say: "Well I don't know. You know you boys been here in settlement a long time. I don't think the government will give it to you. You got tucker, you got flour, you got rice, you got porridge, you got sugar, you got everything, just like wages." But we speak up for wages, we got to see Mr. O'Leary so we write to him and he come to Palm.

"Why you want wages?" He say, "You work long time for tobacco. What you want wages for?" We say: "We want money, want to see what we working for." He say: "I give you four shillings a fortnight, every fortnight."

We glad and happy too. But Mr. O'Leary say: "No gambling now. The minute you gamble and superintendant write a letter saying you gamble, I knock the wages right off and you can go back to food orders." We say: "All right." We promise Mr. O'Leary and we tell all the people not to gamble.

First day we get money Friday. Then Saturday, Sunday and on Monday they are caught gambling, big gambling. Mr. O'Leary say: "Wipe the wages right off." Oh we are sad on the island.

Everybody loses the money and we wait for a while. Then I say: "We will go and try again; we will ask again." So we go to Mr. Simple again and he say: "Right, I give you wages again if you don't gamble but I have to write to Mr. O'Leary."

Mr. O'Leary come back to Palm Island and he say: "Now don't tell me lie this time. I can give you the same wages, four shilling a fortnight but don't gamble. If you get caught gambling I will wipe it off you." We promise "Yes, yes Mr. O'Leary."

But Mr. O'Leary only half way back to Brisbane when they get caught gambling again. I say: "There is going to be a sad day again."

When the council go for the court the superintendant tell us: "Right ho this is gambling so the wages got to stop, no more wages." We go back, caught again, very sad now.

Anyway Mr. O'Leary send back word: "Give them the four bob back again." So we go for two or three months and then they say: "You're gonna get a rise, all the working men." We are all glad and shake hands with one another.

When pay day come we go to see what rise we gonna get. When you go for wages you got to take your hat off and they say: "Sign here. All right Willie Thaiday, four shillings. So and so, four shillings. So and so, four shillings." But now we get seven shillings a fortnight, three shillings rise. By gee we are happy. From that time on he never knock it off. Then it become eight shillings a fortnight up until war broke out.

In 1938 the women used to get an order for endowment. We think: "We will put in for that too." This time we win a victory.

It was a happy day that day when it come. We shake hand all round. The wife to my uncle Palmer, who got a big family, get £21 and she is so excited that the money fall from her hand. That was the first time women get money in the hand. Some get £18, £11, £10 and that night big gamble everywhere, all around the island. And a big mob get caught and they bring them to the court. Mr. Simple say: "I think you all gonna lose the endowment," but when Mr. O'Leary come he say: "No, we can't stop the endowment because it come from the Federal Government, the Commonwealth. That money got to stay."

When war broke out I left the island, left the gang and went to Millaa Millaa for a holiday. From Millaa Millaa we come to

Innisfail. I stay outside nearly three months. Then I go back to Palm Island, back to timber cutting and I take the gang again.

I tried to join the army outside in 1939 but they say: "You can't join the army from Palm Island." So we come back to Palm Island while the ninth, sixth and seventh division Australian boys go overseas.

In 1940, the war get bad and I go to Mackay on a patrol boat for the army. The boat take all the tucker for the army stationed on the islands, Daydream Island and all them. I go round there working for the army. I ask Captain Swain, big army captain: "You put me in army uniform. It is no good this way. You better enlist me in the army." Swain don't want that. He say: "You're from Palm Island." I say: "I don't want to stop in military patrol boat then. You send me to Palm Island." He don't want to send me so I run back to Palm Island.

We stop there working for a while. The war come over this way now and a big mustering start. In 1942, some six hundred Aboriginals from Woorabinda, Palm Island, Yarrabah and Cherbourg all go over to Atherton to pick corn because there is labour shortage. All the other labour went out to Ingham to cut cane but they don't take ordinary white men to cut cane, only Italians from concentration camps.

I stop four years in Atherton picking corn, working for Mr. Harold Collins, Minister for Agriculture. He got a big farm, about 500 acres of corn, and a big mob of reserve men are working there. I stop there right through the war.

In 1945, me and the whole family come to Tully and stop there another four years working on a banana farm. I got my own farm, half share with the boss, fellow called Mr. Jones and I pull my own scrub, grow my own bananas.

When victory day come for the end of the war they have a big float, all kind of float, seventy four I think. I say to Mr. Jones: "What about we try to make Aboriginal float." He say: "That's all right if can make it." So we get a big truck, five ton truck, and I build Gunyah, Myah Myah, on top of it. I use umbrella palms. I got my wife, wife's sister and some old women from Tully. They let their hair down and I leave space for them to peep through Myah Myah and right on top I put a big kookaburra. He look proper champion. Me and my brother in law sing and play the guitar. We sing a corroborree.

And we get two old people with a tin. I say: "Put a stick inside the tin and let it burn through, like you make a spear."

Everybody was happy to see the Aboriginal float come through the streets of Tully from the council office right along the street. I have some old fellows there and they sing out like anything, shake spears, paint up, sing the corroborree, some

make spears and boomerangs and me and Mosely[4] sit in the box singing. We go right around the showgrounds and we win the first prize for the best float. After that I sell the farm, take my half share and come to Halifax.

I stop four years at Halifax cutting cane and working for the council but I went too heavy on grog. One day the policeman say: "Well Willie, you're from Palm Island. You got a removal order from Mr. O'Leary. You got to go back to Palm Island." I was pretty sad but all the same I am happy because Palm Island – that's our home. So the launch come, pick us up and take us over to Palm Island." That was 1950.

We stay on Palm Island, working there. In 1956 I work on the streets making roads but then I go to the farm – cane farm, banana farm. I got three or four acres of bananas, Mr. Bartlam was the superintendant and he say to Mr. Croker[5]: "You better get Willie, see if he can grow bananas for the settlement." Mr. Bartlam say he want to see me in the office so I go and he say: "You got your own farm. What if you grow tem them for the settlement?" I say: "All right," and he pay me ten shillings per week.

1. Eva Geia, National Aboriginal Congress representative for Townsville area.
2. Director of Aboriginal Affairs.
3. Superintendant.
4. Mosely Dickman, Willie's brother in law.
5. Mr. Croker, Overseer.

Palm Island Amateur Boxing Association
Visited Townsville 4th April 1939

Back Row: Eric Lymburner, Mick Ryan, G. Sibley, P. Doyle, G. Barry, M. Miller.
Second Row: J. Harvey, A. Geia, R. Dodd (Manager and Trainer) K. Walsh, J. Davidson.
Floor: E. Ebagoola, J. Sibley, J. Shepherd.

Wedding of Willie and Madge Thaiday; Mick and Cissie Miller, Palm Island, 14th March 1936.

(Left to Right): Alice Sibley (Miro), Mick Miller, Cissie Miller (Sibley), Julian Blanket, Elsie Prior (Sibley), Phyllis O'Malley, Willie Thaiday, Madge Thaiday (Barney), Mick Ryan, Mono Banfield (Bonner).

Queen's Visit Celebrations, Townsville, 1954
(Left to Right): Willie Thaiday, Frank Jack, Sylvia Conway, Bertha Sailor and Sylvia Jack.

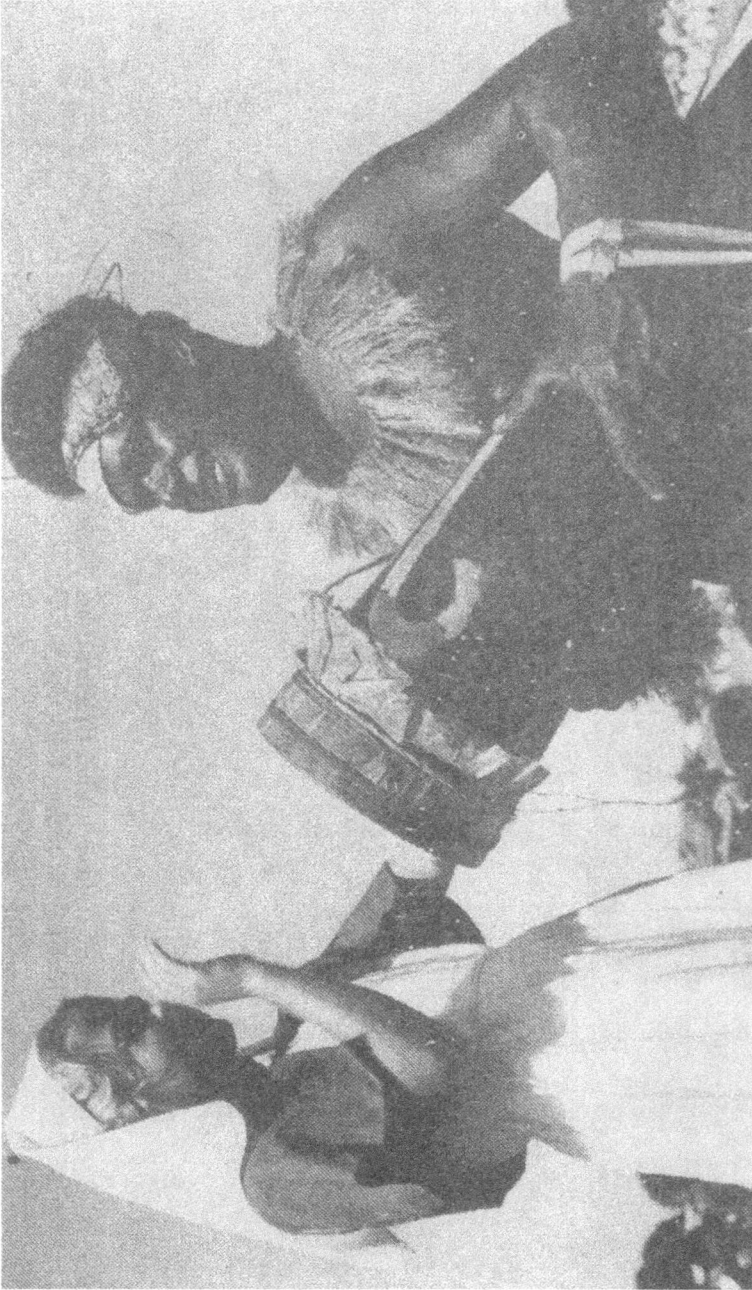

Willie Thaiday at Queen's Visit Celebrations, 1954
(courtesy Townsville City Library)

CHAPTER THREE:

PALM ISLAND (part two)

Everything on Palm Island is the idea of the Superintendant and according to the superintendant we are the last people on earth. When they want anything they sing out: "Jack, Bill, Harry – come and get me them things; get the meat, get the flour, get this, get that." And the moment you refuse, you go to gaol for twenty one days.

The policemen on Palm Island should not be called policemen. They are only trackers from far away inland and they know nothing about law, not a scrap. They never been to school and all they do is what the superintendant tell them. "Can you do this?" "Yes boss." "Can you do that?" "Yes boss." They never say no. Then they come to try to stand over us by the power of the superintendant.

We got to do everything what suit the superintendant, not us and every super that go there got the law in his own mouth. What he say is law and the state government allow them to make the rules.

We know it is wrong but still you can't say nothing because the moment you say something they throw you in gaol. If they say you got to go to gaol you can't say what for and you don't know when you come out. I saw some boys, two or three of them, who spent 18 months without court.

Every white who stop over there got a yardman and the poor yardman got to do everything they tell him to – get our meat, get our rations. When the beef come from town on the boat all the whites get the first serve. They slice all the good parts away for them and only the bones and a little bit of meat is left for all the people on the settlement, fifteen hundred people. Then we all line up to go to the window to get our meat, one by one. Sometimes it is eight o'clock or nine o'clock before we finish at the butcher but if you go home and speak up that you missed the meat you have to go to gaol.

Every time the white people come from Townsville we got to cart their ports up to their place and when they ready to go we got to go and get their ports and put them into the boat again. They are like kings but I don't think even a king is like that. They do better than a queen.

One time I was foreman on the milk. We go milking cows, about forty-six milkers. When we milk them they give first milk to white fellows and the rest of the milk go for us natives for the babies. But for us blacks you got to break it down with water – three gallons of milk you put water in – bring it up to four or five gallons. I do that myself. Mr. Bartlam make me do because I am the foreman.

Another time I made seven big fish traps on Palm Island. It was hard work – you gotta go up in the hills and cut fifty sticks about fourteen or fifteen feet long. I make seven fish traps out of them sticks. Then you bring them over and catch the tide. We caught a lot of fish that way. One day I caught a big groper, weigh nearly 800 pounds, in Frances Creek. Mr. Croker say: "Come in and we will take a photo of the groper to send down to Brisbane for the annual report." But next morning when I go into the settlement to take the photo I find out that Mr. Bartlam is going to be in the photo so they will say that he caught the fish. He caught nothing.

Everything I do they get the credit for. The farming job – vegetables, bananas, lettuce, cabbage, cucumber, radish, carrot. I planted them all but when they are unloaded at the shop they come there like they been working hard. They get their wages for nothing. I planted six hundred coconut trees yet I never tasted one coconut or got any credit for it.

I put a new road in for the banana farm on top of the hill towards Mt Lindsay so the trucks can go up there to get the bananas. We made it with mattocks and pick and shovel. Mr. Taylor who was there didn't know how the hell we did it without a bulldozer.

Around Butler Bay Mr. Croker tried to plough some new ground. He couldn't do it because there were a lot of roots from old trees so he got me to do it. I ploughed all around there and did a good job.

Mr. Croker and Mr. Taylor were trying to plant pawpaw. They do everything back to front but I can't tell them anything because I will go to gaol. Then they ride around in trucks giving orders and getting their money for nothing.

Even them who crawl up to Mr. Bartlam get nothing for it – only a pat on the back.

They treat us like dogs on Palm Island. To them we are only animals but we are human, the same as them and we got feelings the same as them, only trouble is we are coloured. Sometimes I sit down and think: for two hundred years they treat us like that. All our land they take away and we are waiting patiently for them to give it back. They still look down on us. Why do they do that? They are educated; they know good from bad.

They send priests, pastors to our island preaching the gospel of Jesus Christ every Sunday. They rest on the pulpit on Palm Island and preach the gospel to us:

> Thou shalt not kill;
> Must love one another;
> Not to hate one another, not to get hatred.

Why they got to preach to us when we abide by them things. And when the priest turn his back different whites come in and say you can hate one another because they got hatred themselves against us.

I think it is my turn to talk now – all I can do is write it in a book. I not say anything lie about them things because it all happened on Palm Island.

During the war when me and my cousin are working on the farm of Mr. Harold Collins they trust us. He got to go to Brisbane and Canberra now and again for meetings and he leave us there by ourselves to work. Sometimes there are eight of us, sometimes six, sometimes four. We farm, scarify, harrow five hundred acres and we get on very good. Now, if the superintendant on Palm Island reckons we are bad how can we look after the farm for white man, member of Parliament, Minister for Agriculture and Stock? We got no hatred feeling, we know how to treat one another.

Small wages too but I put up with it for four years. I only pull out when I get double pneumonia. When we go to Palm Island Mr. Bartlam might think we are bad but if he got the boot like us during the war he wouldn't stand working for small wages. There must be something good in us.

When I work for Mr. Jones, a good white man, I got three acres bananas myself. I pick the bananas, send the cases to Townsville and sell them here. Everything is all right. And yet when I go to Palm Island Mr. Bartlam class me as no good, as a loafer, can't do the job. Why can't we do the job over there when we do good job on the mainland?

When I am living in Halifax after I come down from Atherton I cut cane with all the good cane cutters – the gun cutters they call them – Doug Jacobs, Arthur Pitt, Wigel Turner. Now what's wrong with that? But back on Palm Island Mr. Bartlam condemn me.

You got to be Under the Act to know the Act. We used to go out to play football to all the outside towns – Ingham, Innisfail, Tully, Mt Isa, Home Hill, Townsville and when we go out from the Island we get strict instruction not to touch drink, must behave ourselves. Just like a mob of kids.

I remember one time we go to Mt Isa and when we get there we are told to go way out from Mt Isa to some old fellow's place to sleep on the ground. He got a lot of bullocks but he got no freezer or anything and the meat is full of flies. So what do we do? We come from Palm Island where we live cleaner than them people outside. We refuse to camp there, all get back in a truck and come back to Mt Isa. We tell police we can't camp there so they make us camp in the police station. Yet we go out to entertain the people, give them sport, only too pleased to get a change from Palm Island. Other footballers they find a good place for them, motel or something like that but we are under the rules of the settlement and the state government no matter where we go.

Same in Ayr, same in Home Hill, same in all them places. And we make good entertainment for the people. In Home Hill we draw the biggest crowd ever been there, make big money. Same night we have a dance but still and all the police must be there, order from Palm Island.

I don't know – we are civilised, we know what to do. Different if we go murder, rape or scrapping but we do nothing of that sort. We only go for football. I don't think in the rest of the world they do like they do for us Aboriginals in Queensland from the settlement. Doesn't matter where we go we belong to the police.

By this time now we should be free a long time. We should have our own business and our children should have their own business but I got ten children in my family, four daughters and six sons and they don't want to take an interest in their lives because they are brought up the wrong way in the settlement, never get good schooling like they do today.

Soon as trouble crop up in the settlement you see so and so minister for the government say something, so and so other minister say something else but they only want to clear themselves and they get out of it by saying all kinds of words against a man – call me communist, militant, black power. It's not that – we are human, got feelings, can think too. And for speaking out against it I get sent from the Island.

Palm Island Football Team
Townsville Sports Reserve (late 1920's or early 1930s)

Aborigines at Queen's Visit, Townsville 1954
Left to Right: Dick Bostock, Jimmy Phillips, Sam Conway, Gerry Hagen.
(courtesy Townsville City Library)

NO VIOLENCE IN REPORTED PALMS RIOT

There had been no damage caused and no violence took place during the reported outbreak of a disturbance at Palm Island Sub-Inspector J. J. Cook said by telephone from the aboriginal settlement Tuesday afternoon.

JUNE 12, 1957.

14.6.57

Seven Palm Island Natives In Custody

Seven handcuffed aborigines were brought ashore by police at Townsville on Thursday after having been transported by a R.A.A.F. crash launch from Palm Island.

19.6.57

25 Aborigines Removed From Palm Island

Twenty-five Palm Island aborigines left Townsville under police escort on the Brisbane mail train last ight.

Department Head To Visit Palm Is.

BRISBANE, June 11.—The Native Affairs director (Mr. C. O'Leary) is to visit Palm Island following Monday's disturbance on the island.

Mr. O'Leary said to-night that a departmental inquiry into the disturbance would be held as soon as possible. He would visit the island but did not know when.

13.6.57

Police Sent To Palm Island

A party of police from Townsville rushed to Palm Island by R.A.A.F. crash launch last night following a report of the outbreak of a disturbance there.

The superintendent of the Palm Island aboriginal settlement (Mr. R. H. Bartlam) asked for assistance at about 6 p.m.

The police party was led by Sub-Inspector J. J. Cooke. Late last night radio-telephone contact could not be made with the island.

11.6.57

47

CHAPTER FOUR:

THE STRIKE

The trouble really start on Palm Island when Mr. Croker interfere with the hygiene gang. The hygiene gang is run by Albie Geia and he got experience with Mr. Garrett who show them how to run it. Mr. Croker come from the bush somewhere and start to tell them what to do. They don't pay Albie the right way so Albie tell them they can stick the money. But Mr. Bartlam don't want that because Mr. Croker is brother in law to him.

One night I see Sonny Sibley, Freddy Clay, George Watson, Billy Congoo, Eric Lymburner and Albie Geia talking in the street but I don't know what for. They say: "Come over here. Listen, we think to make a strike." I say: "What for you make a strike?" They say: "We see if we can strike against Mr. Bartlam."

I don't know anything about the trouble because I am running the banana farm. Anyway I go with them because I am full up with Mr. Bartlam. Any small thing that you do wrong he cut your wages. He is never satisfied. I only get ten shillings a week yet he cut my wages – no wages at all for a whole month, but Mr. Bartlam make sure he get his full wages every fortnight. He don't care about anyone else. They can starve so long as they work for himself and Mr. Croker.

Mr. Bartlam also treat our women very bad. I saw with my own eyes the women who refuse to go and scrub the hospital or the houses of the white officials. They shove them in gaol. The women can't do it because they got to look after their little ones in the home but he won't have it – they still got to do what he want.

When I was there I was a policeman too – got two stripes. In the daytime I work on the farm and night time I got to do duty in the settlement. One day they tell me to escort a girl from gaol to sweep around the office and the street and they give her a bag dress to wear – ordinary sack only they cut the corners where they put the sleeves – all that by Mr Bartlam's instructions. One day I take them and they say they wouldn't do it. Mr. Merton went mad: "Take them back in gaol," he say.

During the strike a lot of our mates double cross us. They come and talk to us; then go back to Mr. Bartlam and tell him what we say.

Mr. Bartlam is not game enough to come out of the office. He lock himself inside with a few blacks who crawl up to him. I know all of them and can name them now.

One time I see Neville Bonner's wife, that's Mona Bonner, the late Mona Bonner and her sister, Jessie Pickle standing together with my wife because they are blood cousins. I hear Neville Bonner's wife call out. "Neville, what are you doing inside Mr. Bartlam's office? You talk to him all the time you big crawler. Come out and help them outside." The women start screaming and they all get sand and throw it inside the windows at Mr. Bartlam.

One part of it we all walk up to the Church of England hall to ask Father Gribble to come out and give us advice about the strike. Father Gribble come out and say to us: "I know you boys; I know your mothers and fathers; I make them married; your children come to me for advice. Well, if you like to strike that is your own business but my advice is to go back, get the tools and start work because you must remember that you have wives and children to feed. You must do the right thing to support them. Go and do the settlement jobs until Mr. O'Leary come. Then you can have a talk to him but my advice to you is go back and do the work." We thank him and walk out but when I come up the road to the office I see all them Mr. Bartlam crawlers walking ahead to the office. They probably tell Mr. Bartlam what we are talking about.

When the strike was over Mr. Bartlam give a recommendation to the government to send Father Gribble away from Palm Island back to Yarrabah mission where he started his early days, after he lived many many years on Palm Island. That's how good Mr. Bartlam is. He is really perfect.

One quiet night all the white police come over when they hear the news. But before that Albie and them fight all the native

50

police and knock them out. Then they ring up for white police and straight away they come over – twelve in a military patrol boat from Townsville. They walk around the village doing nothing. That night another twelve police come over. Every one of them got a gun, a .44 revolver. Mr. Cronin was the Detective Sergeant.

Next night I see Sonny and I say: "By gee, this night is too still. Must be something gonna happen." Sonny say: "No, everything all right. Nothing gonna happen." Everything was peaceful.

Early in the morning, about four o'clock they strike my place – Detective Sergeant Cronin, Inspector Cook and Greg Barry, Senior Sergeant of Police. Mr. Cronin say: "Don't move Willie or you gonna get hurt." I say: "What for?" He say: "You come under arrest." Soon as I come out the door they catch me. They shove me, make me go forward. Detective Cronin say: "Don't try to do any dirty trick else you get hurt."

They slam handcuffs on my hands and we come down to the beach. There is another five coming too and we all seem to reach that boat together. Albie Geia, Billy Congoo, Sonny Sibley, George Watson, Eric Lymburner and Gordon Tapau.

Anyway we walk down to the beach and get into a boat, a flatty. We start to argue then. We say to Greg Barry: "You're not a fair man. Some day this thing fly back to you."

Soon as we pull out a bit I strike out in a big song – island song about our home. The captain, fellow called Mr. Whiting hear us and say: "Who them boys? They can't be going to prison in handcuffs. They seem so happy."

We sing like anything in the military patrol boat. It belong to air force in Townsville. The policemen are on top and machine gun is pointed down to us but while we are in front of machine gun we sing like anything.

When we get on the boat it is nearly daylight. The walky talky is going all the time, talking to people on shore, talking to people in Townsville. They ask them. "How them boys?" They say nothing wrong. They singing like hell here." Mr. Whiting can't get over it.

They wait to arrest us. They think we all wild fellows on boat but we all happy fellows. When eight o'clock come Inspector Cook and Detective Sergeant Cronin ask my wife: "You want to come too?" She say: "Oh yes I like to go." "Roll the swag; take what you can; sit in the same boat with Willie." So women and family come on the same boat. They send the other people after. I got one child about four months old and one grandson. I look from the boat and see them walking on the jetty. I think: "All the family coming. That's all right." We are still in the boat singing like anything. I feel happy. I don't care about my belongings. Everything is lost. Somebody can pick them up. I got no chance to claim them.

The sea was very rough, thirty or forty knot wind. I tell policeman: "You better take my handcuffs off because them kids might fall overboard. I got to watch them." He good sergeant too, take the handcuffs off. I hold my little daughter and all the others Nina, Dulcie, Telle, David, all the little ones squashed up. I sit on the stern and get wet all the way from there to Townsville. The others, Albie and them, inside in handcuffs with policemen guarding them. All of them got .44s on their sides, Just like we do a big murder.

We come to Townsville to the air force wharf and we get off. Police car ready there too. We stop there now to wait for a removal order to come from Mr O'Leary. Four days later the removal order come: "Willie Thaiday, Albie Geia, Sonny Sibley – Woorabinda. Billy Congoo, George Watson, Eric Lymburner – Cherbourg. Gordon Tapau – Bamaga."

Sammy Doolan, Dad Thaiday, Sageare Day, Harrison George

Left to Right: Willie Thaiday, Fred Krause, Ivy Sam, Mrs. Krause, Madge Thaiday

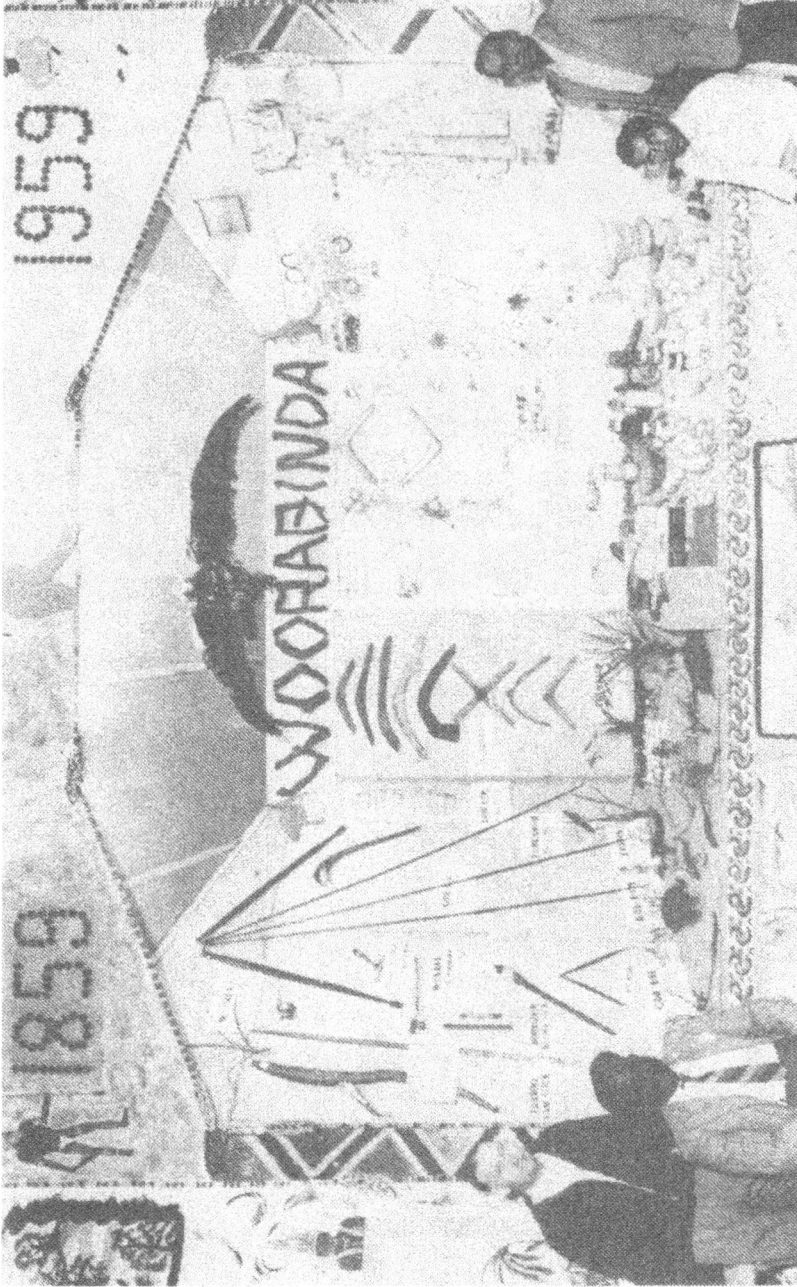

Left to Right: Col Allen. Willie Thaidav. William Rowrow. Clancie Booth

CHAPTER FIVE:

WOORABINDA

When we leave for Woorabinda it is cold as anything and we got no warm clothes, nothing. I come away with only one shirt. We go a day and a night to Rocky. They take me to gaol in Rockhampton, lock me up. My wife too, and all the family was locked up. Then they take me to Woorabinda that same night. Then we get to Duaringa, forty miles from Woorabinda, and we catch a car, Fargo, to take us to Woorabinda.

The sergeant who escort us from Palm Island it still with us at Duaringa. We come Fargo, he come in too. We meet settlement car. Mr Bailey is driver and two native police from Woorabinda. It is really bad drive and we are jammed up like fish in a tin. You got to sit like that all the way and they put the handcuffs on us too. We come to Woorabinda boundary and Mr Bailey say: "If you boys like to run away you can run away now." We are thirteen miles from Woorabinda. We say nothing. He talk smart.

We get to Woorabinda but got no home to sleep so they take me and put me in single men's home. Me and my family was jammed up in one corner of single man's home. I say: "No matter. We put up with it." Them other blokes are all right. They don't come with their families so they sleep anywhere.

Next morning we get up and Mr. Knaggs the superintendant come in and say: "Well Willie there is one old broken home there. You got to find the best way to make it good. We won't give you truck to get timber. We will get all the mattresses for you but you got to take timber on your shoulders."

I see the house. It's got a bark roof and bark wall and I say: "That's no good to me – too dirty, stinking, everywhere proper filthy. I don't care if I have to go to gaol. I will refuse that house. I will go to tell Mr. Knaggs."

Before I left Palm Island they have a show and I win the prize in the competition for good home. I got a good home, good yard, first class everything. I leave a good home on Palm Island. I never do bad on Palm Island you know. We had argument there with superintendant for his wrong doing. He treat you like a dog on Palm – that's why we come here.

Anyway Mr. Shepherd say: "You got to go in that house." I say: "No, I won't take my family to sleep there. I will stay in the boys home." He say: "Please yourself." So we bring all the mattresses down five, six, seven hundred yards. I lump them on my shoulder, one at a time.

I got no relations there you see. I know a lot of people there but no relations who can call me into their home. We got no saucepan, no plate, no spoon, nothing and there are ten in my family. We live that way, eating very little tucker, cooking very little. We only borrow saucepan, borrow plate, borrow spoon. And you have to go to work next morning. They say: "If you no work you go to gaol."

One morning the superintendant call me into the office: "Now you can go out if you like. I give you ten pounds and you can look for a job." Well I can't go. I got all my family there and I try to set up. I say to Albie: "Go on you go first. I stop to make it good for all this family. I go afterwards."

So I stop and get settled down. I stay with single men but all kinds of things happen – swearing and so on. Some old people, belong to wife, come and tell me: "You come over to our house. That house you got not much good. This is house for married man." So we go and stop with them for a few months I think.

I work with the carpenter. I go back to work at one o'clock, supposed to start at half past. Mr. Knaggs talk to Mr. Bailey and say: "He must be a good worker I think." One day he come down to me and say: "You like to go in good home now?"

Inside that new place you can't see for smoke. Somebody made a big fire inside and blacken the place but I go there. We got no pleasant things but we stuck there all the same. My wife go to her cousin house to borrow things. Anyway I clean every thing, scrub the smoke and it come like a good home.

I tell the wife: "I must go, must try to work." So I see Mr. Knaggs but he put me on the farm where we work for nothing, only a piece of tobacco. I say to Mr. Knaggs: "I go look for a job." He say: "Here is ten pounds. You go out."

I go, use ten pounds to pay my train fare to Townsville. I go in Townsville and look around but this place is all grog. Albie and them all here among the drunk people. I say: "I don't think I stop here." I report to railway station: "Any job here on the railway?" They say: "Yes, you got job here but you have to go to gang eighty one." That is way up north at Rangoo, outside Ingham about eighty one miles. Lot of sandflies there. I say: "That's all right. I take it."

When I go up there, there is nothing at all, no modern clothes but I work. First pay I buy something, a little bit. I work there for two months but the the railway run out of money. The inspector say: "They gonna pay off all the temporary blokes and you too Willie. They gonna pay them off from Innisfail right to Townsville. You allowed to leave." That's all right so next day I say to the inspector: "you better write my pass for the train fare. I go to Rocky." He say: "No, you not been here long time. I can't give you pay. You got to pay the ticket. That time it cost eleven pounds, I think, from here to Rocky. I leave the job, go to Rockhampton, then to Woorabinda and start work there again.

Mr. Knaggs see me again. He come down with Sergeant Swan following him. He know me well from Palm Island when he was Senior sergeant there. He say to Mr. Knaggs: "I like to get that fellow for Policeman." Mr. Knaggs say: "Which fellow?" "Willie." "You think he all right?" "Yes, he was policeman on Palm Island; make a good policeman that fellow." So they talk to themselves but I know nothing about it. I see Mr. Bailey and Mr. Knaggs come straight from the building. They call me over. Mr. Knaggs say. "Come here Willie. How did you get that house up like that? I didn't know you had experience as carpenter." "Oh yes I try my best." "You know what, I try and make you policeman. You like to do police job?" "Yes I don't mind." "All right, you leave job here and come and get uniform." So I go, get uniform. In a fortnight's time he come down to the police station again and he tell sergeant Swan: "I gonna give Willie one stripe, make him one stripe sergeant, a corporal." All right; next week come; Knaggs tell Swan: "Give willie another stripe, make him two stripe sergeant." Three weeks come and he say: "Give Willie another stripe, make him three stripe sergeant. He will be second to you now."

I stay there a good while. In 1959 I help the welfare man to make a concert, biggest concert you ever can find, beautiful concert for forty-two young girls. We take it to Baralaba, Theodore, Bulliwallah, Banana, Wowan, Rockhampton.

At Rockhampton they send for me. They tell Mr. Knaggs: "Can Willie come here and dance for us?" All right; everything fixed up; I go down to Rockhampton. For the show they build a special stage at the showground. There was a white bloke there, too Willie Furnell, I think. While we travel down there they announce on the wireless all the time and on the day before the show they take my photo and put it in the Bulletin, the Rockhampton paper, right on the front page. I think: "Gee, I got to dance good now; they gonna look for me."

Father Arthurs was the Catholic priest and I think how to help the mission. Me and the wife very strong Catholics from Palm Island. The church is in the showgrounds at Woorabinda and it got names in every corner, every board in sight, names of young boys and girls: "So and so, so and so lovers only." It spoil the church and hardly anybody go. The Church of England is the same but the Aborigine's Inland Mission all right. The Catholic church was right outside but the Aborigine's Inland Mission and Church of England right inside.

I think to myself: "I will go tell Mr. Knaggs if I can see Mr. O'Leary." He say: "What do you want?" I tell him about the church. He say: "You can see me." I say: "Why do Catholic church stay out there and people draw signs on it. Bring the

Catholic Church right into the heart of the settlement." Mr. Knaggs say: "What do you want to shift the Catholic Church for?

You want to show off?" He make a joke. I say: "Mr. Knaggs, if it is all right to bring up church we start to build it now." He go to see O'Leary himself. O'Leary very strong Catholic. Mr. Knaggs say: "All right. Father Arthurs is very happy: "Willie, you do very good thing. You helping the people."

We start to work on the church now. Two carpenters from Theodore come in. while we make the church I think to myself: "Them people, they might mark the church again." So I say to Mr. Knaggs: "Can you build my home in front of the church, straight in front." He say: "What for? You got a house." My name was good there then so he say. "All right , I put a big on there for you." A new brown one they put up for me, lovely home. We go and get new furniture from Rockhampton. It cost us six hundred pounds. New church and new home. Mass every Sunday. People come from Rocky. Nothing ever go wrong. And I planted trees around the church. If you go to Woorabinda today you can see the same trees.

So I stop there and slacken off. People get jealous and they start to talk about me because they can't do nothing. They been there so long. I say: "I don't want to break their heart." And I tell wife: "I think we might go at Christmas time." We have Christmas at Garden Valley, Mt. Isa line, with my cousin Joe. Everything go all right and Joe say: "You want a job here? You want to stop." This time wife stop and I go back. I sell all the things for one hundred pounds and come back. My wife tell me: "That the last time we ever go to Woorabinda."

I work on the railway as fettler. They very bad people too – always look down on a man. When I try to come up my cousin turn on me, gonna tell the inspector about me. They say this way, that way but it's not true. I say: "We keep going. It don't matter. Some day it gonna be good."

I go on another gang then, Winton section, work there. Fellow there called Allan Bannon say: "I can't see anything wrong Willie." So he come in, talk to Harry Adcock[1] and say: "I think that man there, Willie, is fit for ganger." Harry say: "You better try Scruddick, seven mile out. There is small house there. Family can stay there." I work in Hughenden in winter and when I finish there I come to Scrudddick. As temporary ganger I work section from Garden Valley to Hughenden. Harry Adcock come to my section and say: "That man work on railway before?" I say: "No, only work at Rangoo but never do much. They paid me off."

I work there and then put for transfer to Prairie and I get Prairie. There I on longer section, seven miles this way and seven miles that way. I come right up to Worrea where there is big double loop where the train change. I work four years at Hughenden, almost as long at Prairie, then I look for transfer. Tully come up and I put in for Tully. No trouble – I get Tully. My wife get a native home on the coast and she is very glad I come. That is 1964 and I work in Tully 64, 65, 66, 67, 68.

In 1968 I get stroke. Doctor say: "That the finish of work." Then I go on invalid pension. Never work no more.

[1] Harry Adcock – Railway Inspector.

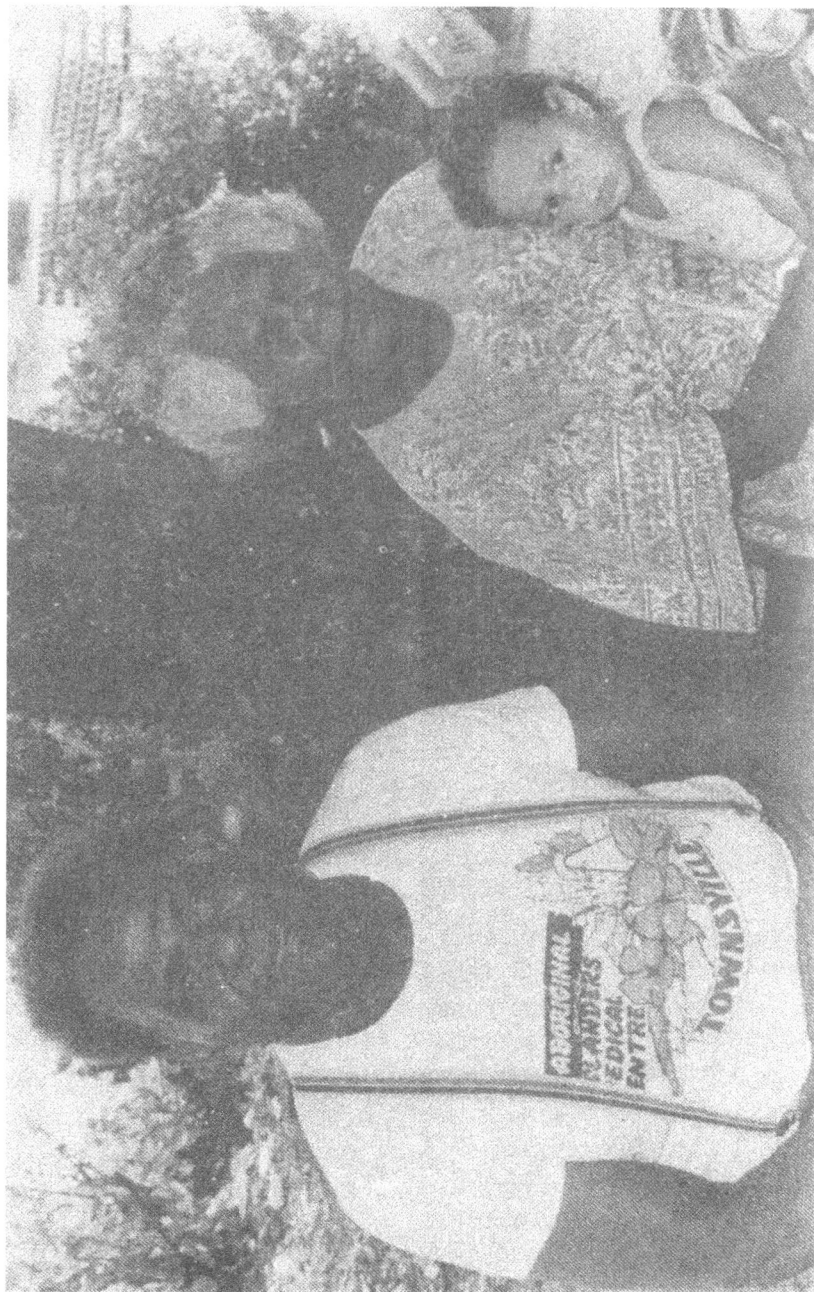

Willie, Madge and grandson: Palm Island 1979

CHAPTER SIX:

PALM ISLAND REFLECTIONS

Palm Island is a place that I like to live all my life but Palm Island is not today like it was before. We were really friendly people on Palm Island; everybody enjoyed themselves; dancing nearly every night. You see the old people out in the moonlight walking around the village, no electric light, only oil and kerosene lamps. One house might invite them to go and have tea and the grounds you see old fellow playing accordion, singing songs. You have island dancers from Torres Strait and people from way out west, all parts of Australia, all full blood doing big corroborees from all the different tribes – Clumpoint, Babinda, Cairns, Kuranda, Bowen, Cooktown, Laura, Lumma Lumma – all the different dances. They were good and we were very happy. Nobody worrying for anything although we got no money, no wages.

But today there is a lot of crook work – I see with my own eyes. People come in with broken chins, split heads, gunshot and knife wounds but they do nothing about it although we got the white police over there. Them things happen every day on Palm Island. Yet here in Townsville if a small thing happen they go to Stuart Creek prison for a few months. In Palm Island they can get out of it because the white police over there don't try to see them things. But why?

Fancy a boat taken to the mainland, come back full of grog and nothing said by the police. Police in Townsville here won't let you carry guns in the street. Over there they allow it. Why? Why do they let you fire guns and wound people – it happen every week. Why don't they send them people to Stuart Creek?

You got the black market over there but nothing is said. Here in Townsville if a fellow is drinking grog on the footpath or carry grog in the street or black market, goodness gracious the police are on him straight away. The young people over there grow up thinking no law against grog. You see young girls under fifteen drunk, young boys under sixteen carry guns in the street. Why do things go like that when they got white police over there? Haven't they got any law for them? Here in Townsville even the white girls are not allowed to drink under age – the police will pick them up quick as lightning, but in Palm Island they let them go.

Them things can be stopped but the people there can't say nothing because the manager is in charge. He is in charge of everything – even the council is worked by the manager. I think they don't want to spoil it for the state government that is behind it all and so they can say to the world that Palm Island is still uncivilised: "Let them murder one another so the world can see that Palm Island is uncivilised." Palm Island is not uncivilised. Palm Island make a beautiful home if only they got police over there who can stand over troubles. It was a tourist island one time – people going by the hundreds – but today white fellows are too afraid to go over.

They want somebody to go over there to work hard to beautify the island, to work with his whole heart to do the place up – grow the coconut trees, almond trees, ash trees. They like to work here in Townsville for Aboriginal people but they are not game enough to go over there to do something for them people because you got to work hard. Here they go around with a pencil and a book, going to fix things for Aboriginals, do that for Islanders. But they are nothing.

I been all around the tourist islands – Whitsunday Island, Green Island, Hayman Island, Daydream, Southmore, Lindeman, Brampton – Palm Island can develop and be like them places. It is not too late. You can do them things.

Now a while back there was a boy over there making big money. He got $22,000. He bought a land rover and a boat. That money – where does he get it from? The black market. Everything over there they sell on the black market – wine $50, beer $15, rum $50, flagon $40. The police from Townsville raid the place and question him – only doing there duty no doubt. Then they arrest him, bring him in Townsville and take all the things from him in the island.

The trouble is he get that money for himself. He could have done better for the island. If he got any sense he can start a business, a co-operative store for all the island, a big super refreshment store over there for all the people and the visiting people. He had enough money but he went on and on and that's how he got caught.

All the same I reckon it is fair thing to give the boy them things back again. The money go around the island, he does nobody harm, he struggle for them things, and he never buy stupid things – he buy something for his own use. And they allow the black market. Why don't they have a case against the black market if it is the black market.

The police over there don't stop the black market – they stop home everyday and work in the office. The state government is behind all that. They do nothing. Why don't they stop it in the first place? According to Palm Island Aboriginals and elsewhere the state government forget about them but it don't forget them – it just don't want to develop them.

The manager over there don't tell the police to stop them, he just let it go. The whites are only there for their own pocket and they get pay for nothing. Close the store when they like; they don't care a damn what the people are doing over there – they don't care if they starve. Better get them shifted out from the island and get the good natives to run the place themselves.

Another thing I wonder is why the case not held in Townsville. I don't think they are game enough to have the case because the state government will fall in and white people outside will come to know. Some white people got a feeling for us and they would jump at the case and show up the state government as a crook. It is crook every time you look.

Whenever you say something they got point to cover it and they always win because they are the government. We never win – we are just the rubbish blacks to them. Yet they are wrong. And according to God's Law which we all believe they are doing crimes all the time. They break the ten commandments – I don't think they Christian at all.

[1] Prison

CERTIFICATE OF EXEMPTION No. 21/50

THIS IS TO CERTIFY that .... Jack Barry ....

of .... Madison

is hereby exempt from the Provisions of "The Aboriginals Preservation and Protection Acts, 1939 to 1946" and the Regulations thereunder, subject to the conditions specified hereunder:—

....

....

....

(Date) .... 4th January, 1950.

....
Director of Native Affairs

A condition of the granting of this Certificate of Exemption is that such Certificate of Exemption shall, upon revocation, be delivered up to the Director.

N.B.—The Director may, at any time, revoke any Exemption and thereupon the provisions of this Act shall apply to such aboriginal as if no Exemption had ever been granted.

69

MEMORANDUM

16th April 1969

To District Officers,
CAIRNS & MAREEBA.

Dear Sir,

Dick Drumduff D329. of Chillagoe is travelling to both Cairns & Mareeba and is expected back in Chillagoe in approximately 6 weeks time.

Drumduff is a waster and it would be appreciated if only small amounts were given for pocket money.

A/c 175 AT 31-2-69. #/981·72

Yours faithfully

DISTRICT OFFICER
CHILLAGOE

70

Please Visit

http://www.undertheact.com

www.ingramcontent.com/pod-product-compliance
Lightning Source LLC
Chambersburg PA
CBHW070930270326
41927CB00011B/2806